Eid al-Adha

Festivals Around the World

Words in **bold** can be found
in the glossary on page 24.

Book Life
King's Lynn
Norfolk PE30 4LS

ISBN: 978-1-78637-030-3

©This edition was published in
2018. First published in 2017.

All rights reserved.
Printed in Malaysia.

A catalogue record for this book
is available from the British Library.

Written by:
Grace Jones

Edited by:
Charlie Ogden

Designed by:
Matt Rumbelow

Eid al-Adha
Festivals Around the World

Hello, my name is Noor.

When you see Noor, she will tell you how to say a word.

What Is a Festival?

A festival takes place when people come together to celebrate a special event or time of the year. Some festivals last for only one day and others can go on for many months.

Some people celebrate festivals by having a party with their family and friends. Others celebrate by holding special events, performing dances or playing music.

What Is Islam?

Islam is a **religion** that began over 1,000 years ago in the Middle East. **Muslims** believe in one God, called Allah, whom they pray to in a mosque which is a Muslim place of **worship**.

A mosque in Abu Dhabi.

Muslims read a holy book called the **Qur'an**. The Qur'an is Allah's word and instructs people on how to practise their **faith**. An **imam** teaches people about Allah's word and leads prayers in a mosque.

Noor says:
MOSK (Mosque)
KUR-AN (Qur'an)

What Is Eid al-Adha?

Eid al-Adha is a festival celebrated by Muslims in September of every year. The festival marks the end of the **Hajj**, which is the journey to **Mecca**, in Saudi Arabia, that every Muslim should make at least once in their lives.

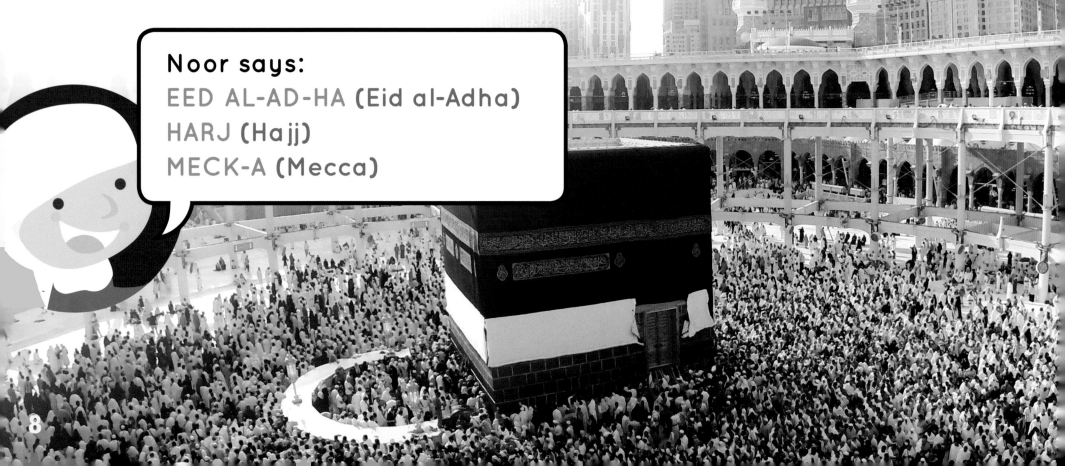

Noor says:
EED AL-AD-HA (Eid al-Adha)
HARJ (Hajj)
MECK-A (Mecca)

During Eid al-Adha, Muslims remember the importance of **obeying** Allah. **Pilgrims** throw pebbles at a wall in Mecca, hold prayers at a mosque and visit their family and friends.

Eid al-Adha is celebrated for two to four days, depending on which country you live in.

The Story of Eid al-Adha

A long, long time ago, there was a wise man called **Ibrahim**. One night, when Ibrahim was fast asleep, Allah appeared to him in a dream. He asked Ibrahim to **sacrifice** his son, **Ishmail**, to show his faith and obedience to him. When he awoke, Ibrahim decided to follow Allah's orders.

The devil also spoke to Ibrahim and told him to go against Allah and spare his son.

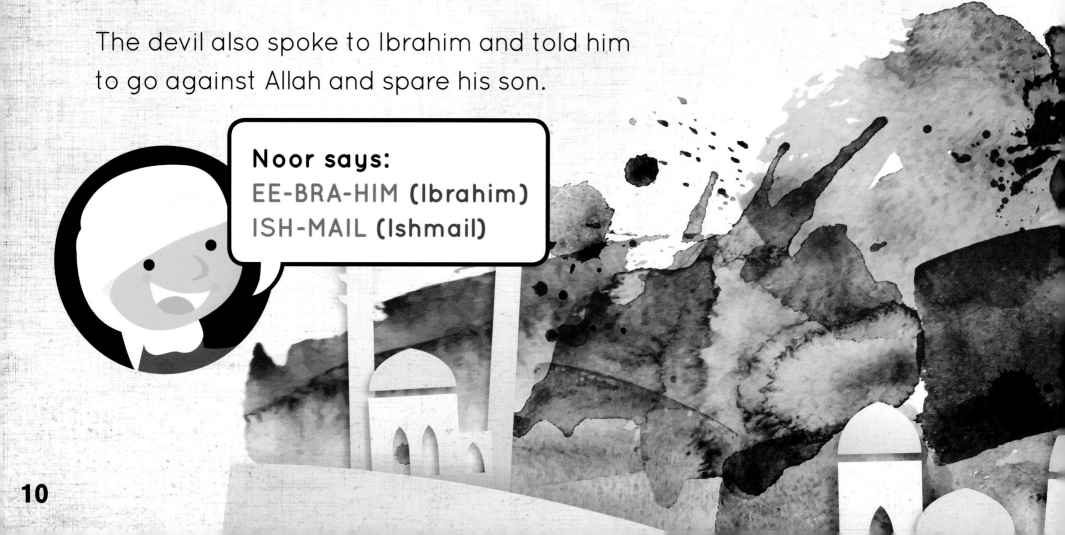

Noor says:
EE-BRA-HIM (Ibrahim)
ISH-MAIL (Ishmail)

Faithful Ibrahim ignored the devil and took Ishmail to a town near the holy city of Mecca. Just as Ibrahim was about to sacrifice his son, a voice called from above; it was Allah, who told him to stop. In Ishmail's place, Allah gave him a lamb to sacrifice instead. Ibrahim's obedience to Allah was celebrated throughout the land.

Ibrahim's faith in Allah is celebrated at Eid al-Adha.

The Hajj

The festival of Eid al-Adha takes place on the last day of the Hajj. The Hajj is a pilgrimage to Mecca that Muslims must make once in their lifetime, as long as they have the money to and they are healthy.

Every year, over two million Muslims from around the world travel to Mecca.

The Hajj takes place in the last month of the Islamic year. There is a large building in the middle of a mosque in Mecca, called the Kaaba, around which Muslims must walk seven times.

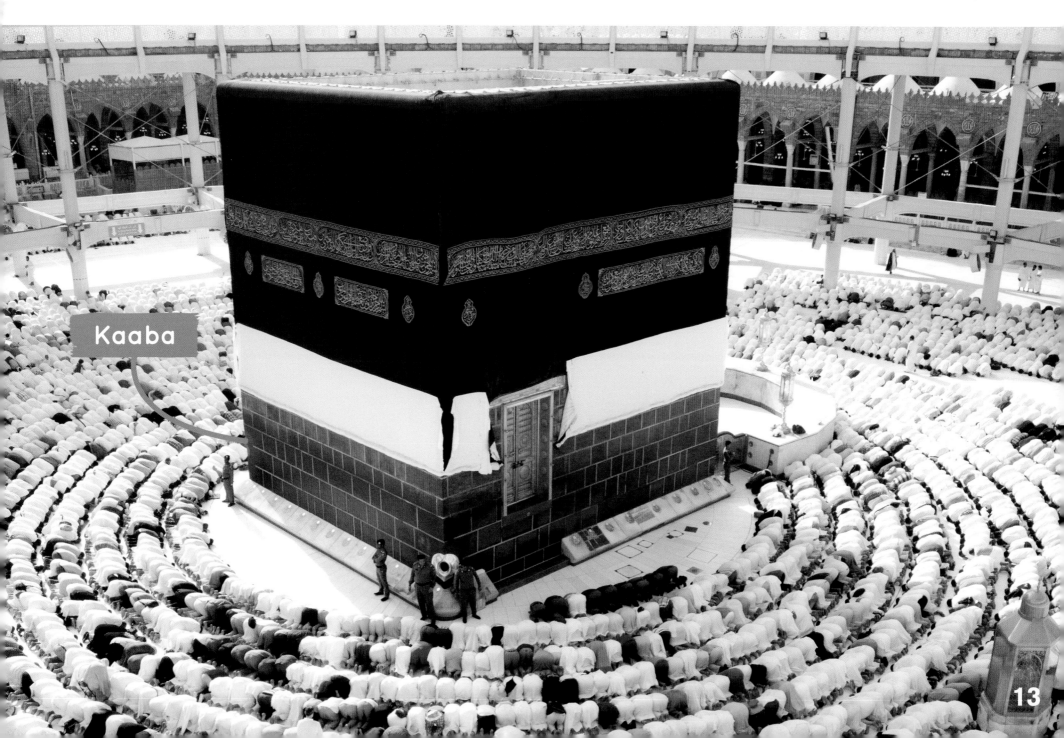

Kaaba

Festival of Sacrifice

Muslims celebrate Ibrahim's obedience to Allah during the festival. This is why Eid al-Adha is also called the Festival of Sacrifice.

Muslims who have made the journey to Mecca begin Eid al-Adha by throwing pebbles at a stone wall called the Jamarat. They believe that there were three pillars where the devil tried to persuade Ibrahim not to follow Allah's word. The Jamarat represents those three pillars.

Prayer and Worship

Other Muslims who have not made the pilgrimage to Mecca start the day early and put on new clothes. They go to their nearest mosque to take part in morning prayers.

It is a time when people ask Allah to forgive them for anything they have done wrong. Many Muslims also visit and pray for their families and friends who are no longer with them.

Gifts and Charity

After prayers finish, everyone continues the celebrations with their family and friends. Many children receive gifts of toys and sweets from adults.

Eid al-Adha also celebrates the importance of looking after one another and giving **charity** to those who are less fortunate. Muslim families usually sacrifice a cow or a goat and give some of the meat to people who do not have enough money to buy it.

19

Festive Food

Eid al-Adha is also known as the 'Salty Eid' because of the amount of salty foods that are eaten at the festival. Meat that has been sacrificed, usually beef, goat or lamb, is eaten as part of the main meal during Eid.

Rice dishes, such as biryani, are very popular in India during Eid al-Adha. A biryani is a dish traditionally made with rice, lamb and spices.

Biryani

Noor Says...

Eid al-Adha

"EED AL-AD-HA"

A Muslim festival.

Hajj

"HARJ"

A journey to Mecca taken by Muslims.

Ibrahim

"EE-BRA-HIM"

A messenger of God (Allah).

Ishmail
"ISH-MAIL"
Ibrahim's son.

Mecca
"MECK-A"
The most holy city for Muslims, found in Saudi Arabia.

Mosque
"MOSK"
A Muslim place of worship.

Qur'an
"KUR-AN"
The Islamic holy book that contains the writing of Allah's word.

Glossary

charity an individual or group of people who help those in need

faith great trust in someone or something

imam a religious teacher of the Islamic faith

Muslims people who follow the religion of Islam

obeying following someone's instructions

pilgrims people who go on a religious journey or pilgrimage

religion a set of beliefs based around a god or gods

sacrifice to kill an animal or human as an offering to God

worship a religious act, such as praying

Photo Credits

Index

Photocredits: Abbreviations: l-left, r-right, b-bottom, t-top, c-centre, m-middle.
Front Cover & 1 – L: India Picture, R: DiversityStudio, bg: Allies Interactive. 2 – Yarygin, 4 – Tom Wang, 5 – Zurijeta, 6 – Fitria Ramli, 7 – MidoSemsem, 8 – ZouZou, 9 – nisargmedia.com, 12 – shahreen, 13 – Zurijeta, 14 – ZouZou, 15 – abahujang, 16 – Zurijeta, 17 – Smailhodzic, 18 – Antonina Vlasova, 19 – Smailhodzic, 20 – Nickola_Che, 21 – Dinu's.
Images are courtesy of Shutterstock.com. With thanks to Getty Images, Thinkstock Photo and iStockphoto.